Clocks

By

Jerome K. Jerome

Copyright © 2013 Read Books Ltd.
This book is copyright and may not be
reproduced or copied in any way without
the express permission of the publisher in writing

British Library Cataloguing-in-Publication Data
A catalogue record for this book is available from the
British Library

Jerome K. Jerome

Jerome Klapka Jerome was born in Walsall, England in 1859. Both his parents died while he was in his early teens, and he was forced to quit school to support himself. Jerome worked for a number of years collecting coal along railway tracks, before trying his hand at acting, journalism, teaching and soliciting. At long last, in 1885, he had some success with *On the Stage – and Off,* a comic memoir of his experiences with an acting troupe. Jerome produced a number of essays over the following years, and married in 1888, spending the honeymoon in "a little boat" on the Thames.

In 1889, Jerome published his most successful and best-remembered work, *Three Men in a Boat*. Featuring himself and two of his friends encountering humorous situations while floating down the Thames in a small boat, the book was an instant success, and has never been out of print. In fact, its popularity was such that the number of registered Thames boats went up fifty percent in the year following its publication. With the financial security provided by *Three Men in a Boat,* Jerome was able to dedicate himself fully to writing, producing eleven more novels and a number of anthologies of short fiction.

In 1926, Jerome published his autobiography, *My Life and Times.* He died a year later, aged 68.

CLOCKS.

There are two kinds of clocks. There is the clock that is always wrong, and that knows it is wrong, and glories in it; and there is the clock that is always right—except when you rely upon it, and then it is more wrong than you would think a clock *could* be in a civilized country.

I remember a clock of this latter type, that we had in the house when I was a boy, routing us all up at three o'clock one winter's morning. We had finished breakfast at ten minutes to four, and I got to school a little after five, and sat down on the step outside and cried, because I thought the world had come to an end; everything was so death-like!

The man who can live in the same house with one of these clocks, and not endanger his chance of heaven about once a month by standing up and telling it what he thinks of it, is either a dangerous rival to that old established firm, Job, or else he does not know enough bad language to make it worth his while to start saying anything at all.

The great dream of its life is to lure you on into trying to catch a train by it. For weeks and weeks it will keep the most perfect time. If there were any difference in time between that clock and the sun, you would be convinced it was the sun, not the clock, that wanted seeing to. You feel that if that clock happened to get a quarter of a second fast, or the eighth of an instant slow, it would break its heart and die.

It is in this spirit of child-like faith in its integrity that, one morning, you gather your family around you in the passage, kiss your children, and afterward wipe your jammy mouth, poke your finger in the baby's eye, promise not to forget to order the coals, wave at last fond adieu with the umbrella, and depart for the railway-station.

I never have been quite able to decide, myself, which is the more irritating to run two miles at the top of your speed, and then to find, when you reach the station, that you are three-quarters of an hour too early; or to stroll along leisurely the whole way, and dawdle about outside the booking-office, talking to some local idiot, and then to swagger carelessly on to the platform, just in time to see the train go out!

As for the other class of clocks—the common or always-wrong clocks—they are harmless enough. You wind them up at the proper intervals, and once or twice a week you put them right and "regulate" them, as you call it (and you might just as well try to "regulate" a London tom-cat). But you do all this, not from any selfish motives, but from a sense of duty to the clock itself. You want to feel that, whatever may happen, you have done the right thing by it, and that no blame can attach to you.

Clocks

So far as looking to it for any return is concerned, that you never dream of doing, and consequently you are not disappointed. You ask what the time is, and the girl replies:

"Well, the clock in the dining-room says a quarter past two."

But you are not deceived by this. You know that, as a matter of fact, it must be somewhere between nine and ten in the evening; and, remembering that you noticed, as a curious circumstance, that the clock was only forty minutes past four, hours ago, you mildly admire its energies and resources, and wonder how it does it.

I myself possess a clock that for complicated unconventionality and light-hearted independence, could, I should think, give points to anything yet discovered in the chronometrical line. As a mere time-piece, it leaves much to be desired; but, considered as a self-acting conundrum, it is full of interest and variety.

I heard of a man once who had a clock that he used to say was of no good to any one except himself, because he was the only man who understood it. He said it was an excellent clock, and one that you could thoroughly depend upon; but you wanted to know it—to have studied its system. An outsider might be easily misled by it.

"For instance," he would say, "when it strikes fifteen, and the hands point to twenty minutes past eleven, I know it is a quarter to eight."

His acquaintanceship with that clock must certainly have given him an advantage over the cursory observer!

But the great charm about my clock is its reliable uncertainty. It works on no method whatever; it is a pure emotionalist. One day it will be quite frolicsome, and gain three hours in the course of the morning, and think nothing of it; and the next day it will wish it were dead, and be hardly able to drag itself along, and lose two hours out of every four, and stop altogether in the afternoon, too miserable to do anything; and then, getting cheerful once more toward evening, will start off again of its own accord.

I do not care to talk much about this clock; because when I tell the simple truth concerning it, people think I am exaggerating.

It is very discouraging to find, when you are straining every nerve to tell the truth, that people do not believe you, and fancy that you are exaggerating. It makes you feel inclined to go and exaggerate on purpose, just to show them the difference. I know I often feel tempted to do so myself—it is my early training that saves me.

Clocks

We should always be very careful never to give way to exaggeration; it is a habit that grows upon one.

And it is such a vulgar habit, too. In the old times, when poets and dry-goods salesmen were the only people who exaggerated, there was something clever and *distingue* about a reputation for "a tendency to over, rather than to under-estimate the mere bald facts." But everybody exaggerates nowadays. The art of exaggeration is no longer regarded as an "extra" in the modern bill of education; it is an essential requirement, held to be most needful for the battle of life.

The whole world exaggerates. It exaggerates everything, from the yearly number of bicycles sold to the yearly number of heathens converted—into the hope of salvation and more whiskey. Exaggeration is the basis of our trade, the fallow-field of our art and literature, the groundwork of our social life, the foundation of our political existence. As schoolboys, we exaggerate our fights and our marks and our fathers' debts. As men, we exaggerate our wares, we exaggerate our feelings, we exaggerate our incomes—except to the tax-collector, and to him we exaggerate our "outgoings"; we exaggerate our virtues; we even exaggerate our vices, and, being in reality the mildest of men, pretend we are dare-devil scamps.

We have sunk so low now that we try to *act* our exaggerations, and to live up to our lies. We call it "keeping up appearances;" and no more bitter phrase could, perhaps, have been invented to describe our childish folly.

If we possess a hundred pounds a year, do we not call it two? Our larder may be low and our grates be chill, but we are happy if the "world" (six acquaintances and a prying neighbor) gives us credit for one hundred and fifty. And, when we have five hundred, we talk of a thousand, and the all-important and beloved "world" (sixteen friends now, and two of them carriage-folks!) agree that we really must be spending seven hundred, or at all events, running into debt up to that figure; but the butcher and baker, who have gone into the matter with the housemaid, know better.

After awhile, having learned the trick, we launch out boldly and spend like Indian Princes—or rather *seem* to spend; for we know, by this time, how to purchase the seeming with the seeming, how to buy the appearance of wealth with the appearance of cash. And the dear old world—Beelzebub bless it! for it is his own child, sure enough; there is no mistaking the likeness, it has all his funny little ways—gathers round, applauding and laughing at the lie, and sharing in the cheat, and gloating over the thought of the blow that it knows must sooner or later fall on us from the Thor-like hammer of Truth.

And all goes merry as a witches' frolic—until the gray morning dawns.

Truth and fact are old-fashioned and out-of-date, my friends, fit only for the dull and vulgar to live by. Appearance, not reality, is what the clever dog grasps at in these clever days. We spurn the dull-brown solid earth; we build our lives and homes in the fair-seeming rainbow-land of shadow and chimera.

To ourselves, sleeping and waking there, *behind* the rainbow, there is no beauty in the house; only a chill damp mist in every room, and, over all, a haunting fear of the hour when the gilded clouds will melt away, and let us fall—somewhat heavily, no doubt—upon the hard world underneath.

But, there! of what matter is *our* misery, *our* terror? To the stranger, our home appears fair and bright. The workers in the fields below look up and envy us our abode of glory and delight! If *they* think it pleasant, surely *we* should be content. Have we not been taught to live for others and not for ourselves, and are we not acting up bravely to the teaching—in this most curious method?

Ah! yes, we are self-sacrificing enough, and loyal enough in our devotion to this new-crowned king, the child of Prince Imposture and Princess Pretense. Never before was despot so blindly worshiped! Never had earthly sovereign yet such world-wide sway!

Man, if he would live, *must* worship. He looks around, and what to him, within the vision of his life, is the greatest and the best, that he falls down and does reverence to. To him whose eyes have opened on the nineteenth century, what nobler image can the universe produce than the figure of Falsehood in stolen robes? It is cunning and brazen and hollow-hearted, and it realizes his souls ideal, and he falls and kisses its feet, and clings to its skinny knees, swearing fealty to it for evermore!

Ah! he is a mighty monarch, bladder-bodied King Humbug! Come, let us build up temples of hewn shadows wherein we may adore him, safe from the light. Let us raise him aloft upon our Brummagem shields. Long live our coward, falsehearted chief!—fit leader for such soldiers as we! Long live the Lord-of-Lies, anointed! Long live poor King Appearances, to whom all mankind bows the knee!

But we must hold him aloft very carefully, oh, my brother warriors! He needs much "keeping up." He has no bones and sinews of his own, the poor old flimsy fellow! If we take our hands from him, he will fall a heap of worn-out rags, and the angry wind will whirl him away, and leave us forlorn. Oh, let us spend our lives keeping him up, and serving him, and making him great—that is, evermore puffed out with air and nothingness—until he burst, and we along with him!

Burst one day he must, as it is in the nature of bubbles to burst, especially when they grow big. Meanwhile, he still reigns over us, and the world grows more and more a world of pretense and exaggeration and lies; and he who pretends and exaggerates and lies the most successfully, is the greatest of us all.

The world is a gingerbread fair, and we all stand outside our booths and point to the gorgeous-colored pictures, and beat the big drum and brag. Brag! brag! Life is one great game of brag!

"Buy my soap, oh ye people, and ye will never look old, and the hair will grow again on your bald places, and ye will never be poor or unhappy again; and mine is the only true soap. Oh, beware of spurious imitations!"

"Buy my lotion, all ye that suffer from pains in the head, or the stomach, or the feet, or that have broken arms, or broken hearts, or objectionable mothers-in-law; and drink one bottle a day, and all your troubles will be ended."

"Come to my church, all ye that want to go to Heaven, and buy my penny weekly guide, and pay my pew-rates; and, pray ye, have nothing to do with my misguided brother over the road. *This* is the only safe way!"

"Oh, vote for me, my noble and intelligent electors, and send our party into power, and the world shall be a new place, and there shall be no sin or sorrow any more! And each free and independent voter shall have a bran new Utopia made on purpose for him, according to his own ideas, with a good-sized, extra-unpleasant purgatory attached, to which he can send everybody he does not like. Oh! do not miss this chance!"

Oh! listen to my philosophy, it is the best and deepest. Oh! hear my songs, they are the sweetest. Oh! buy my pictures, they alone are true art. Oh! read my books, they are the finest.

Oh! *I* am the greatest cheesemonger, *I* am the greatest soldier, *I* am the greatest statesman, *I* am the greatest poet, *I* am the greatest showman, *I* am the greatest mountebank, *I* am the greatest editor, and *I* am the greatest patriot. *We* are the greatest nation. *We* are the only good people. *Ours* is the only true religion. Bah! how we all yell!

How we all brag and bounce, and beat the drum and shout; and nobody believes a word we utter; and the people ask one another, saying:

"How can we tell who is the greatest and the cleverest among all these shrieking braggarts?"

And they answer:

"There is none great or clever. The great and clever men are not here; there is no place for them in this pandemonium of charlatans and quacks. The men you see here are crowing cocks. We suppose the greatest and the best of *them* are they who crow the loudest and the longest; that is the only test of *their* merits."

Therefore, what is left for us to do, but to crow? And the best and greatest of us all, is he who crows the loudest and the longest on this little dunghill that we call our world!

Well, I was going to tell you about our clock.

It was my wife's idea, getting it, in the first instance. We had been to dinner at the Buggles', and Buggles had just bought a clock—"picked it up in Essex," was the way he described the transaction. Buggles is always going about "picking up" things. He will stand before an old carved bedstead, weighing about three tons, and say:

"Yes—pretty little thing! I picked it up in Holland;" as though he had found it by the roadside, and slipped it into his umbrella when nobody was looking!

Buggles was rather full of this clock. It was of the good old-fashioned "grandfather" type. It stood eight feet high, in a carved-oak case, and had a deep, sonorous, solemn tick, that made a pleasant accompaniment to the after-dinner chat, and seemed to fill the room with an air of homely dignity.

We discussed the clock, and Buggles said how he loved the sound of its slow, grave tick; and how, when all the house was still, and he and it were sitting up alone together, it seemed like some wise old friend talking to him, and telling him about the old days and the old ways of thought, and the old life and the old people.

The clock impressed my wife very much. She was very thoughtful all the way home, and, as we went upstairs to our flat, she said, "Why could not we have a clock like that?" She said it would seem like having some one in the house to take care of us all—she should fancy it was looking after baby!

I have a man in Northamptonshire from whom I buy old furniture now and then, and to him I applied. He answered by return to say that he had got exactly the very thing I wanted. (He always has. I am very lucky in this respect.) It was the quaintest and most old-fashioned clock he had come across for a long while, and he enclosed photograph and full particulars; should he send it up?

From the photograph and the particulars, it seemed, as he said, the very thing, and I told him, "Yes; send it up at once."

Three days afterward, there came a knock at the door—there had been other knocks at the door before this, of course; but I am dealing merely with the history of the clock. The girl said a couple of men were outside, and wanted to see me, and I went to them.

I found they were Pickford's carriers, and glancing at the way-bill, I saw that it was my clock that they had brought, and I said, airily, "Oh, yes, it's quite right; bring it up!"

Clocks

They said they were very sorry, but that was just the difficulty. They could not get it up.

I went down with them, and wedged securely across the second landing of the staircase, I found a box which I should have judged to be the original case in which Cleopatra's Needle came over.

They said that was my clock.

I brought down a chopper and a crowbar, and we sent out and collected in two extra hired ruffians and the five of us worked away for half an hour and got the clock out; after which the traffic up and down the staircase was resumed, much to the satisfaction of the other tenants.

We then got the clock upstairs and put it together, and I fixed it in the corner of the dining-room.

At first it exhibited a strong desire to topple over and fall on people, but by the liberal use of nails and screws and bits of firewood, I made life in the same room with it possible, and then, being exhausted, I had my wounds dressed, and went to bed.

In the middle of the night my wife woke me up in a great state of alarm, to say that the clock had just struck thirteen, and who did I think was going to die?

I said I did not know, but hoped it might be the next-door dog.

My wife said she had a presentiment it meant baby. There was no comforting her; she cried herself to sleep again.

During the course of the morning, I succeeded in persuading her that she must have made a mistake, and she consented to smile once more. In the afternoon the clock struck thirteen again.

This renewed all her fears. She was convinced now that both baby and I were doomed, and that she would be left a childless widow. I tried to treat the matter as a joke, and this only made her more wretched. She said that she could see I really felt as she did, and was only pretending to be light-hearted for her sake, and she said she would try and bear it bravely.

The person she chiefly blamed was Buggles.

In the night the clock gave us another warning, and my wife accepted it for her Aunt Maria, and seemed resigned. She wished, however, that I had never had the clock, and wondered when, if ever, I should get cured of my absurd craze for filling the house with tomfoolery.

The next day the clock struck thirteen four times and this cheered her up. She said that if we were all going to die, it did not so much matter. Most likely there was a fever or a plague coming, and we should all be taken together.

Clocks

She was quite light-hearted over it!

After that the clock went on and killed every friend and relation we had, and then it started on the neighbors.

It struck thirteen all day long for months, until we were sick of slaughter, and there could not have been a human being left alive for miles around.

Then it turned over a new leaf, and gave up murdering folks, and took to striking mere harmless thirty-nines and forty-ones. Its favorite number now is thirty-two, but once a day it strikes forty-nine. It never strikes more than forty-nine. I don't know why—I have never been able to understand why—but it doesn't.

It does not strike at regular intervals, but when it feels it wants to and would be better for it. Sometimes it strikes three or four times within the same hour, and at other times it will go for half-a-day without striking at all.

He is an odd old fellow!

I have thought now and then of having him "seen to," and made to keep regular hours and be respectable; but, somehow, I seem to have grown to love him as he is with his daring mockery of Time.

He certainly has not much respect for it. He seems to go out of his way almost to openly insult it. He calls half-past two thirty-eight o'clock, and in twenty minutes from then he says it is one!

Is it that he really has grown to feel contempt for his master, and wishes to show it? They say no man is a hero to his valet; may it be that even stony-face Time himself is but a short-lived, puny mortal—a little greater than some others, that is all—to the dim eyes of this old servant of his? Has he, ticking, ticking, all these years, come at last to see into the littleness of that Time that looms so great to our awed human eyes?

Is he saying, as he grimly laughs, and strikes his thirty-fives and forties: "Bah! I know you, Time, godlike and dread though you seem. What are you but a phantom—a dream—like the rest of us here? Ay, less, for you will pass away and be no more. Fear him not, immortal men. Time is but the shadow of the world upon the background of Eternity!"

www.ingramcontent.com/pod-product-compliance
Lightning Source LLC
Chambersburg PA
CBHW031819110426
42743CB00057B/1076